To my children Tara, Peter and Sarah-Jess.

CREATIVE RIBBON EMBROIDERY

SALLI VAN RENSBURG

Quilters' Resource

ACKNOWLEDGEMENTS

I would like to thank my family and students whose encouragement and enthusiasm made this book possible.

To Lianne Cox for her photography work.

To Camina Turgel for styling.

To Viv Askin for transferring my handwritten script to computer.

To Alex Groen who neatened up my drawings and helped me with the artwork.

To Tara van Rensburg, my wonderful daughter, who spent hours patiently modelling the wedding dresses and hat.

To Wilmington Enterprise for numerous frames.

To my cousin Lesley Delport who encouraged my sewing in South Africa.

Copyright Salli van Rensburg © 1994

ISBN 0-9629056-2-3

First edition, first impression 1994

Quilters' Resource

P.O. Box 148850
Chicago, Illinois 60614
(312) 278-5695 Fax (312) 278-1348

Typeset by 4-Ways DTP Services, Cape Town
Production, design and cover design by Wim Reinders & Associates, Cape Town
Reproduction by Hirt & Carter, Cape Town
Printed and bound by National Book Printers, Goodwood

Salli van Rensburg (née Hudson-Beck) was born in Harare, Zimbabwe, where she matriculated with honours in needlework and art at Arundel School. She travelled all over the world for 4 years playing professional tennis, representing Zimbabwe in the Federation Cup and playing at Wimbledon.

From an early age, she showed an interest in all forms of needlework. Her Granny Jess started her off with embroidery, tapestries and cross stitch, and her mother taught her various patchwork styles. While living in America for 2 years where she played tennis, she attended several patchwork and smocking classes. After marrying and moving to Cape Town, where she had three children, her interest in needlework continued. The family emigrated to Australia, where she attended classes with Shirley Bibbings, learning shadow applique, and continuing her interest in patchwork and many other crafts.

She now lives with her family in Johannesburg, where she has a needlework shop and studio and teaches daily.

Her cousin Lesley Delport has been a source of great encouragement and inspiration to her.

CONTENTS

*President Nelson Mandela pictured with
the author when he visited the Creative Needlework
exhibition in 1992*

INTRODUCTION

I first discovered silk ribbon embroidery several years ago through a dear friend of mine from Australia, and I had no idea what a wonderful form of embroidery it would prove to be. Kaye Pyke's book on the different techniques of satin ribbon work inspired me to combine silk and satin ribbon together with free-style crewel stitches. It is exciting to experiment with the wonderful range of coloured ribbons available to the embroiderer; silk, satin, velvet, rayon, polyester and moiré taffeta – and to combine them with some of today's beautiful embroidery threads.

There is a difference between silk ribbon embroidery and satin ribbon. The silk ribbon is very soft and pliable, going through the fabric easily like embroidery thread, whereas the satin ribbon is first worked by hand to form the flowers or leaves, and then sewn onto the fabric.

This book contains a lovely cross-section of ideas for the ribbon work – from clothing to tea-cosies, clocks to towels and cushions, to framed work and hat boxes. Do not feel constrained by the designs in this book; feel free to experiment with different combinations. What I love about this sort of work, is that one can create one's own ideas and designs from the basic techniques and stitches that are illustrated in this book.

Sitting doing handwork is very therapeutic, and has a calming effect on one, and it can be done anywhere – on a plane, in a train, waiting for appointments or children, or just sitting relaxing at home in front of a fire or television.

Ribbon work is surprisingly fast. You will be amazed how quickly you can create something in such a short space of time. The era of the "throwaway" society is passing, and we are now looking for products that last and that we can hand down to our children and grandchildren. We can create and make our own heirlooms.

I am so excited about writing this book. I hope the new ideas and stitches in it will give you lots of pleasure and enjoyment.... but, be warned, once you start, you won't stop!

Happy stitching.

Salli

1
MATERIALS AND EQUIPMENT

SILK RIBBON
Pure silk ribbon has been used in the projects in this book. It is softer and more pliable than any other type of ribbon available, and it comes in various colours and widths. The majority of the flowers are worked with 3.5mm ribbon as I find it more versatile. It is available in three different widths: 2mm, 3.5mm and 7mm.

SATIN RIBBON
Satin ribbon is freely available from most haberdashery and needlework shops in various colours and widths. It has a shine on one side, and is matt on the other side, giving an attractive two-tone effect on some of the roses. I tend to use the 14mm the most – for a finer effect use the 8mm or 10mm width. For the large Victorian roses and bridal gowns, use the 25mm width.

MOIRÉ TAFFETA RIBBON
The moiré taffeta ribbon is the same on both sides, and has been used for some of the large Victorian roses. It is available in a wide range of colours and widths – I have only used the 25mm width.

NEEDLES
Chenille needles are essential for the silk ribbon embroidery. They have a large eye with a sharp point, and are available in mixed packs sizes 18-24.

Embroidery crewel needles No. 7, 8 and 9 are used for the embroidery in this book, with the exception of the bullion stitch and the satin ribbon roses, for which straw needles No. 7 and 8 are required.

FABRICS
Never use poor quality fabrics for handwork – it is not worth putting all your time and effort into it, if it is not going to last. I tend to use natural fabrics for all my work, such as pure cotton, seeded cotton, linen, lawn, or pure silk. Make sure that your fabric is not stiff and hard, as harsh, abrasive fibres will shred the ribbon. For all the work in this book, other than the clothing, muslin has been used behind the fabric, as it holds the work firmly and gives more body to the finished item, as well as providing a neat beginning and finish.

SCISSORS
A sharp pair of small pointed embroidery scissors are essential, as the ribbon will snag if they are blunt, plus dressmaker's scissors are needed for cutting the fabric.

HOOPS
A hoop is very important in ribbon embroidery. If you are a bit awkward at first, persevere, and you will soon get used to it. For the silk ribbon embroidery, the hoop must be small enough for your thumb and index finger to reach the middle, as you need to control the ribbon while stitching. The most successful hoop size is 10-15 cm (4-6").

For the satin ribbon work, you can use a larger hoop. Generally I use a hoop size that fits in the whole design. When you have silk, satin and embroidery together, you would work your silk and embroidery stitches first on the small hoop – then move onto the larger hoop for the satin ribbon work. Make sure your fabric is taut in the hoop – this prevents the stitches from puckering up the fabric, and helps to keep them even and the ribbon flat.

TRACING AND PREPARATION
When tracing onto your background fabric, use a traditional 2B pencil, as it gives a nice fine line. Remember to press lightly, otherwise your work will become very grubby with lead. Use a piece of muslin the same size, and then tack them together, with the muslin underneath. Always tack from the centre out, as this will prevent any puckering or rippling. If you are using a very dark fabric that you cannot see through to trace, use dressmaker's carbon. This gets placed between the background fabric (coloured side facing down onto the fabric) and the pattern. When tracing the pattern, press quite firmly, allowing the carbon to transfer onto the fabric. Tack the muslin behind.

Knitwear requires a different method of tracing. First photocopy your design from the book and pin it to your garment. Tack the pattern through the paper and garment using small running stitches in machine cotton. Remove the paper carefully, tearing through the stitches, leaving your design in tacking stitches on your garment.

You are now ready to begin – relax and enjoy it. If you make a mistake, don't worry. It's not a train smash! Rather cut it out, and start again with new ribbon. It is very difficult to unpick mistakes and virtually impossible to rework the ribbon.

IMPORTANT POINTS FOR SILK RIBBON

THREADING

Silk ribbon is surprisingly easy and quick; don't be frightened of it. Relax, start creating and have fun. You may use most basic embroidery stitches successfully with the silk ribbon. It should be kept short – between 30-35cm is ideal. Any longer, and it starts to fray and look very tatty.

Thread the silk ribbon through the eye of the needle, now pierce this end of the ribbon with the point of the needle (5mm from the end). Pull down on the long end of the ribbon, and you will firmly lock the ribbon into the eye of the needle (see diagram A). This keeps the ribbon from slipping out of the eye of the needle, and you also don't waste any ribbon.

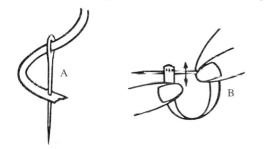

MANIPULATING

Most stitches depend on the ribbon being flat, so manipulate your ribbon. This is achieved by holding the ribbon firmly under the left thumb and sliding the needle under the ribbon backwards and forwards, applying upward pressure on the ribbon with the needle. This should flatten the ribbon (see diagram B).

If the silk ribbon is creased before you begin sewing, set your iron on 'silk' and iron it, but do not iron once you have worked your stitches.

BEGINNING AND ENDING

When starting, make a little backstitch into the muslin, leaving a tail, then pierce it with your first stitch of embroidery. If you have no muslin, make a neat knot. When ending, you can either make two or three backstitches onto the muslin, or weave the ribbon behind the stitches at the back of the work, taking great care not to drag the stitches of the more loosely tensioned ribbon stitches.

It is ideal to have several chenille needles handy, and to thread each one up with the different colours you are going to use. It saves having to keep cutting the ribbon off the needle each time you change colour.

CLEANING

The best results are obtained by dry cleaning, but as this becomes rather expensive after a while, I tend to hand wash 99% of all my work. I would suggest a good quality wool washing solution, and cold water. Should any pencil marks or stains remain, try a soft toothbrush on the stained area. Rinse, and roll it up in a dry, clean towel to remove any excess water. With the work facing down, press the background fabric dry. NEVER iron the ribbon and never leave your work in the water too long, as this can cause colour leakage.

3
BASIC SILK RIBBON STITCHES

LAZY DAISY STITCH

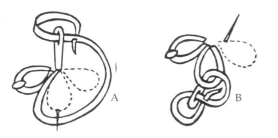

Bring the ribbon out through the fabric, and hold it with your thumb to the left. Make a loop, and re-insert the needle at the starting point, making sure your ribbon is under the needle. Pull through the centre of the loop and secure it with a tiny stitch over the ribbon.

LOOPED DAISY STITCH

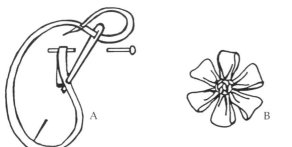

Bring the ribbon through the fabric and manipulate it so it lies flat on the fabric. Depending on the size of the petal, pin over the ribbon. Bring the ribbon back over the pin and push the needle through the centre of the ribbon at the starting point (see diagram A). Make all your petals first and complete your French or Colonial Knots in the centre before removing the pins.

BULLION LAZY DAISY

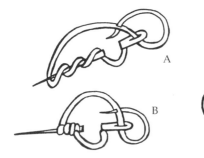

This is a variation of the Lazy Daisy. Work your Lazy Daisy Stitch, but do not pull your needle through; instead, make a small Bullion Stitch, wrapping your ribbon around the point of the needle two or three times. Hold the bullion firmly with your left thumb and index finger and pull the needle through. Remember to keep your thread taut and tight before anchoring the bullion.

COLONIAL KNOT

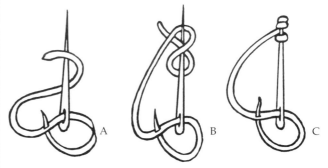

This knot is the best one for silk ribbon work, as it sits nicely on the fabric, and is firmer than other knots. The silk is wound around the needle to form the Figure 8. Bring the needle up through the fabric, and hold the ribbon in your left hand. Slip the point of the needle over and under the ribbon (diagram A), then wrap the ribbon over the needle (diagram B), creating a figure 8. Insert the needle into the fabric close to where it emerged (diagram C), and pull the ribbon taut, to form a firm knot before passing to the back of the fabric.

IRIS STITCH

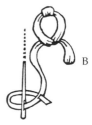
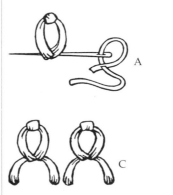

Work a Lazy Daisy Stitch, and bring the ribbon through the fabric on the lower right of the Lazy Daisy. With the back of the needle, so as not to pierce the ribbon, slip the needle under the Lazy Daisy and anchor it on the lower left hand side. Work a Colonial Knot in the centre of the Lazy Daisy Stitch.

FLY STITCH

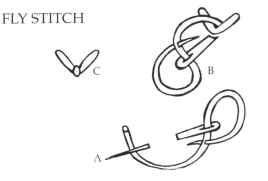

Bring the silk ribbon through at the top left, and hold it down with your left thumb. Insert the needle down to the right on the same level, a little distance from where the silk ribbon emerged. Take a small stitch downwards, to the centre with the ribbon under the needle (diagram A). Pull through and anchor by taking a tiny stitch over the ribbon (diagram B).

INVERTED LEAF STITCH

Bring the ribbon through at the top left of the shape, and making a sloping stitch follow the diagram making sure that you lay the ribbon flat and push the needle back through the centre of it.

INVERTED STAB STITCH

Bring the ribbon up through the fabric and manipulate it so it lies flat on the fabric. Push the needle back through the centre of the ribbon and pull gently, so that the ribbon just curls over the tip.

LOOP STITCH

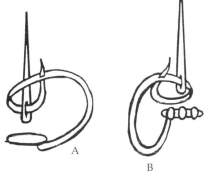

Bring the ribbon out through the fabric and insert it back in a short distance away, leaving a loop. Keep repeating as many times as required. Do not worry if the ribbon twists and turns.

MOCK BULLION

Make a stab stitch, and with the back of your needle wrap the ribbon around the stab stitch four or five times, moving along the stitch. Anchor at the end of the stab stitch.

STAB STITCH

Bring the ribbon out through the fabric at point 'a' and take the ribbon down at point 'b'.

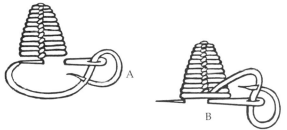

ROUMANIAN

Bring the silk ribbon through at the top left, and hold it down with your thumb. Insert the needle to the right on the same level, and bring it up in the middle with the ribbon under the needle (diagram A). Pull through and take a tiny stitch over the ribbon, bringing your needle up on the left (diagram B).

13

4
BASIC CREWEL STITCHES

BACKSTITCH

Bring the thread up through the fabric, then take a small backward stitch through he fabric. Bring the needle up again a little in front of the first stitch. Repeat, inserting the needle into the same point where it first came through.

BULLION ROSEBUD

Work a 7-twist Bullion Stitch in the middle, and on each side work a 10-twist Bullion Stitch.
Depending on the size required, whatever the number of twists needed for the middle bullion, you add 3 extra twists for each side, eg. 7, 10 & 10 or 8, 11 & 11, etc.

BULLION STITCH

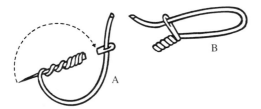

Using a straw needle, make a Backstitch the size of the bullion required, bringing the point of the needle back to where you first came out, do not pull the needle right through. Twist the thread around the point of the needle, as many times as required to fill the space of the backstitch. Hold onto the bullion with your thumb and index finger, and pull your needle through. Still holding the bullion firmly in place, insert your needle back into the fabric as in diagram B. Work the bullion with your finger until it lies flat.

BUTTONHOLE BAR

Make two parallel stitches across the top of the fabric, bringing your needle through where you began. Work your Buttonhole Stitches around the loose stitches without picking up the background fabric.

BUTTONHOLE STITCH

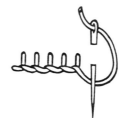

Bring the needle out on the lower line, and insert the needle in position (as per diagram) in the upper line, making a straight stitch downwards, with the thread under the needle. Pull the stitch to form a loop and repeat.

BUTTONHOLE WHEEL
This stitch is done in the same way as your Buttonhole Stitch. Begin on the outer edge of the circle or wheel; remember to work from the middle outwards as shown in the diagram.

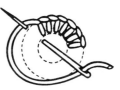

CHAIN STITCH

Bring the thread out at the bottom of the line you are going to work. Hold the thread with your thumb to the left and make a loop. Insert the needle into the centre of this loop and repeat the same process. In this way, a chain of loops is formed.

CORAL STITCH

This stitch is worked from right to left. Pull the thread out and lay it along the line, hold it down with your left thumb. Take a small stitch under the line and thread and pull through as in the diagram.

EXTENDED FLY STITCH

Bring the thread through at the top left, and hold it down with your thumb. Insert the needle at the same level a short distance away and take a small stitch downward to the centre with the thread under the needle, making a "V". Pull through and insert the needle in, however long you want the tail to be, as per diagram.

EXTENDED FRENCH KNOT

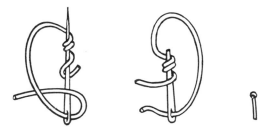

Bring the thread through at the required position, and hold the thread taut with your left hand. Place the needle on top of the thread and wrap the thread round the needle two or three times. Insert the needle whatever distance is required from the exit point.

FEATHER STITCH

Bring the thread through at the top centre, and hold it down with the left thumb, and on the same level a little to the right, insert the needle and take a small stitch down to the centre, keeping the thread under the needle. For the next stitch, insert the needle a little to the left on the same level and take a stitch down to the centre, always remembering to keep the thread under the needle.

FRENCH KNOTS

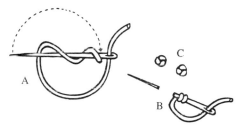

Bring the thread through at the required position, and hold the thread taut with your left hand. Place the needle on top of the thread and wrap it round the needle two or three times. Insert it close to where the thread first emerged. See arrow in diagram A.

LEAF STITCH

Bring the thread through at the top left of the shape, and making a sloping stitch, follow the diagram: out at point a, in at point b; out at point c, in at point d; out at point e; and so on.

RAISED STEM STITCH

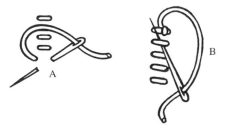

15

Make a ladder of parallel stitches as per diagram A. Bring your thread through at the top right hand side of the ladder. Bring your thread over and under the first parallel stitch. Do not catch the fabric. Continue down the ladder, taking one stitch at a time as per diagram B. Several rows of Raised Stem can be worked, depending on the width of your parallel stitches. Always start at the same end for a neat, even stitch.

ROLLED STEM STITCH

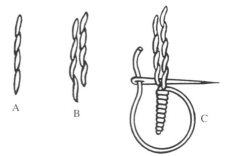

Make two rows of Stem Stitch close together. Bring your thread through at the beginning and take your needle under both rows of the Stem Stitch. Do not catch the fabric. Continue repeating this process as per diagram C, keeping your stitches close together to make a tight roll.

RUNNING STITCH

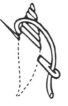

Bring the thread up through the fabric and pass the needle over and under the fabric. The stitches should be even.

SATIN STITCH
Work straight stitches closely together across the shape. Do not make the stitches too long, as they catch easily and pull out of shape.

SPIDER'S WEB STITCH

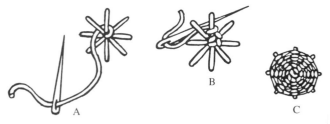

Make a foundation of eight spokes as in diagram A. Bring the thread up in the middle of the spokes and pull through. Pass your needle under two spokes. Do not pick up the background fabric. Pass your needle back one spoke, forward two as per diagram B. Carry on going round and round, until all the spokes are covered. Remember to pull the thread tightly to the centre to accent your spokes.

SPLIT STITCH

With an even number of threads, make a Backstitch, and bring the needle up between the strands, splitting it.

STEM STITCH

Work from left to right, taking even, slanting stitches along the line, as per diagram.

TWISTED CHAIN STITCH

Start the same way as ordinary Chain Stitch, but instead of inserting the needle at the starting point, insert it close to the last loop, making a slanting stitch, as per diagram.

VERTICAL SPIDER'S WEB STITCH

Make a ladder of parallel stitches as per diagram A. Bring your thread through at the top left hand side of the ladder. Pass your needle under the first parallel stitch. Do not catch the fabric. Now go back one spoke, forward two, back one, forward two, as per diagram B. Always start at the same end.

WHIPPED BACKSTITCH

Make a Backstitch, and with a second thread, whip it over and under each stitch. Do not catch the background fabric.

WHIPPED CHAIN STITCH

Make a row of Chain Stitch and with a second thread, whip over and under each stitch. Do not catch the background fabric.

5
COMBINATION STITCHES FOR SILK RIBBON FLOWERS

AGAPANTHUS

Work the leaves and stems in Stem Stitch using 2 strands of green embroidery thread. The flowers are worked in 2 strands of blue/violet thread using Extended Fly Stitch, with the small "V" on the outside of the circle and the long tail going into the small hole in the centre. Make a little French Knot inside every "V", using one strand of the same thread.

BLEEDING HEART

Work the stems in Backstitch using 2 strands of green embroidery thread. The flowers are three inverted Stab Stitches in red silk ribbon. Work the middle one first, and then one on either side, coming out in the same hole at the top, and fanning it out at the bottom. Work the leaves using green silk ribbon in Fly Stitch and then make a Stab Stitch in the middle of the "V". The calyx is worked in Stab Stitch using green silk ribbon. Work 3 extended French Knots at the bottom of the flower in one strand of yellow embroidery thread.

CORNFLOWER

Work the stems in Stem Stitch, using two strands of green embroidery thread. Use 5 Inverted Stab Stitches for the flowers, using blue silk ribbon. Work away from the centre point. The buds are worked in blue silk ribbon, using Lazy Daisy Stitch. Work Fly Stitch in green silk ribbon for the base of the bud. The leaves are worked in green silk ribbon in Inverted Stab Stitch. Make the centre of the flowers with 1 strand of yellow embroidery thread, making a twenty-twist Looped Bullion Stitch in the centre, with a ten-twist Bullion coming out of the middle.

DAFFODILS

Work the stems and leaves of the daffodils in Stem Stitch, with 2 strands green embroidery thread. The trumpet is worked using 4 or 5 Buttonhole Stitches in two strands of yellow embroidery thread going into the same hole at the top of the stem. With yellow silk ribbon, work 4 Lazy Daisy Stitches or 4 Inverted Stab Stitches going away from the base of the trumpet.

SHASTA DAISY

Draw a circle for the centre of your daisy, and working around the circle in white silk ribbon, from the centre out, make 12 Inverted Stab Stitches. Fill the centre with French Knots using two strands of yellow embroidery thread or you can make Colonial Knots in silk ribbon. The stems are worked in a Whipped Backstitch using two strands of green embroidery thread. The leaves are worked in long Inverted Stab Stitch in green silk ribbon, with Feather Stitch worked on the top in one strand of matching thread. The centre of the buds are bullions using two strands of green embroidery thread, with mock bullions in matching silk ribbon fanning away from the centre.

DAISY
Looped Daisy:

Work the stems in Whipped Backstitch with two strands of green embroidery thread. The leaves are Bullion Stitch using the same colour thread.

To make the flower, draw a small circle in the centre of the daisy and make six Looped Daisy Stitches in white silk ribbon. Leave all six pins in place and using two strands of yellow or charcoal embroidery thread, fill the centre with French Knots. Remove the pins.

DELPHINIUM

Work the stems in Coral Stitch and the leaves in Roumanian Stitch, using 2 strands of green embroidery thread. To work the flowers, and using a blue, white or apricot silk ribbon, work up the stems, using Lazy Daisy Bullion Stitch. Work left petal first, then right, then left, then right, until you have reached the top of the stem.

Finish off the flower stalk using a few well-placed Colonial Knots.

FORGET-ME-NOTS

Work the stems and leaves in Stem Stitch using two strands of green embroidery thread.

To work the flowers, make the centre first using yellow silk ribbon and work one Colonial Knot. Work a circle of five Colonial Knots in blue silk around.

FUCHSIAS

The stem of the fuchsia is worked in Backstitch using 2 strands of green embroidery thread. The fuchsia is worked in two colours, the back petals being darker and the centre petals lighter. Use silk ribbon and work in Inverted Stab Stitch. Work the calyx and the leaves in green silk ribbon, using Inverted Stab Stitch. Make the stamens of the flowers in Extended French Knots, using 1 strand of the same coloured thread as the darker silk ribbon of the flower.

GYPSOPHILA

Make the stems using 2 strands of green embroidery thread and work in Stem Stitch. At the top of the stem, make five or six Stab Stitches. Make a Colonial Knot at the end of each Stab Stitch, using No. 8 white candlewicking thread. Continue the knots until they fan out into a mushroom shape.

HONEYSUCKLE

Work the stem in Backstitch using two strands of green embroidery thread. Work 4 Lazy Daisy Stitches for the petals using 1 strand maroon embroidery thread. You can work the leaves in either Inverted Stab Stitch using green silk ribbon, or in Lazy Daisy Stitch using two strands of green embroidery thread.

   To make the stamens, use 1 strand of yellow thread and work 3 Extended French Knots from the centre of each flower.

HYACINTH
Work the stems in Coral Stitch, using 2 strands of embroidery thread and the leaves in Stem Stitch, using the same thread. To make the flowers, work Colonial Knots, using silk ribbon, on either side of the stem as illustrated in the diagram. Work the

bottom knots loosely, making the knots tighter as you work up the stem, so that the shape looks like a Christmas tree.

IRIS

Work the stems and leaves in Chain Stitch using two strands of green embroidery thread. Make your Iris Stitch at the top of the stem in silk ribbon, working a Colonial Knot in the centre in either ribbon or 2 strands of embroidery thread.

JASMINE

Work the stems first in Whipped Backstitch, using 2 strands of green embroidery thread. Make the flower stems next in Inverted Stab Stitch using dark pink silk ribbon. Draw a dot in the centre of the jasmine flower and work 5 Inverted Stab Stitches in white silk ribbon, working from the centre outwards. Work one Extended French Knot coming out of the centre of the flower, using 2 strands of yellow embroidery thread. The jasmine buds are worked in dark pink silk ribbon, by making an Inverted Stab Stitch and at the bottom of the stitch, working a small Lazy Daisy Bullion Stitch. The leaves are Inverted Stab Stitches, worked in green silk ribbon.

LAVENDER
Work the branches of the lavender, starting at the top of the stem and work in Feather Stitch using 2 strands of green

embroidery thread. Into each "V" work a Mock Bullion in silk ribbon.

LILIES

Work the stems in Stem Stitch using two strands of green embroidery thread. With the same thread, work the leaves in Satin Stitch embroidering across the width of the leaf. Work two Buttonhole Bars in a "V"shape at the top of the stem using two strands of embroidery thread. Lastly, work your Extended French Knots coming out of the "V" using 1 strand of yellow thread.

ORCHIDS

Work the stems in Stem Stitch, and the leaves in Leaf Stitch using two strands of green embroidery thread. Make a small circle in the centre of the flower, and in a light pink silk ribbon, work 5 or 6 Inverted Stab Stitches from the edge of the circle outwards. With a dark pink silk ribbon, work four Looped Daisy Stitches inside the circle.

PERIWINKLE

Work the stems in Coral Stitch using 2 strands of green embroidery thread, and with the same thread, work your leaves in Lazy Daisy Stitch.

Work the flowers by making 5 Stab Stitches for each flower. Position these along the stem as shown in the diagram. Finish the 5 Stab Stitches off with a Colonial Knot, worked in blue silk ribbon.

PEACH BLOSSOM

The stems are worked in Chain Stitch using 2 strands of green embroidery thread. The twirly-whirly leaves are worked in Chain Stitch using 1 strand of green thread. The Peach Blossom flowers are worked in Inverted Stab Stitch using apricot silk ribbon. The centres are embroidered with French Knots using 1 strand of apricot embroidery thread.

ROSES
Spider's Web Rose

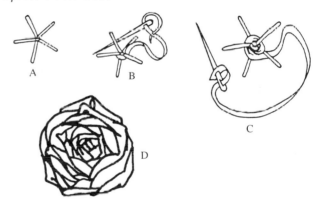

Working outwards and using 3 strands of embroidery thread, make 5 Stab Stitches from the centre point of your rose (diagram A). Bring your silk ribbon up through the centre of the 5 spokes (you may start anywhere), weaving in an anti-clockwise direction, over and under the spokes (as per diagrams B and C). Allow your ribbon to twist and turn and remember to keep the tension loose. Keep working in the circular movement until the spokes are covered.

Colonial Knot Rose
Make 3 Colonial Knots in the centre of your rose using silk ribbon. Keep them close together to form a triangle. Start

between any two knots and work Stem Stitch around the knots clockwise, remembering not to pull the ribbon too tightly. Carry on going round and round until you have the rose the size you want it.

Crossed Chain Rose

Make a very small, loose Lazy Daisy Stitch in the centre of your rose. Using silk ribbon and working in an anti-clockwise direction, start the Crossed Chain Stitch. Work in a circular movement until you have the size of rose you want.

Koeksister Rose

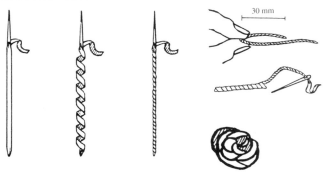

Bring your silk ribbon up through the middle of your rose. Twist the needle between your thumb and finger, causing the ribbon to twist. Insert the tip of the needle back into the fabric (close to where you came out – but not in the same hole) and pull through very slowly and gently, stopping when you have a perfect rose. Secure the rose in the centre by embroidering a few French Knots using 1 strand of embroidery thread, either yellow or a colour of your choice.

Leaf Stitch Rose

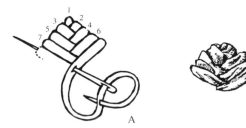

Work the petals as per numbering in diagram A, in Inverted Stab Stitch, using the technique of the Leaf Stitch. Note that it takes on a fan shape. For an added, more natural effect, use a darker ribbon at the top going into a lighter colour at the bottom.

Mock Bullion Rose

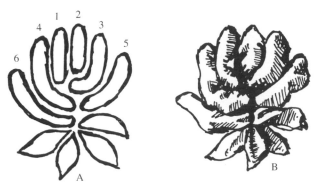

Work the petals as per numbering in diagram A, using the "Mock Bullion" Stitch. Then, using your Inverted Stab Stitch, make four base petals.

Dog Rose

Working with 7mm width silk ribbon, make five Inverted Stab Stitches, working from the centre out and making sure you do not pull the stitch all the way through the ribbon, but leave a slight curl at the end of the stitch. Fill the centre with one yellow Colonial Knot in silk ribbon. Then with two strands of yellow embroidery thread, make an Extended French Knot half-way up each petal on top of the ribbon.

Pre-Gathered Rose

Bring the ribbon up through the fabric in the centre of the rose. With 1 strand of embroidery thread in a colour matching the silk on a straw needle, bring it up next to the silk ribbon. Make a small running stitch along the edge of the ribbon for about 10-15cm. Gather it up and make a circle with it;

make two layers if you want to. Take both needles to the back of the fabric and end off the silk ribbon. With your one strand of embroidery thread, catch the rose into position around the edge.

Rosebuds

Make a Lazy Daisy in the silk ribbon. Open up the centre and make a Colonial Knot inside. A Fly Stitch in green silk ribbon underneath makes a lovely calyx.

SALVIA

Make one Inverted Stab Stitch in silk ribbon. With two strands of green embroidery thread, make an Extended Fly Stitch, the "V" snugly fitting around the base of your Inverted Stab Stitch. Come up into the middle of the silk and make a Stab Stitch into the "V" of the Fly Stitch. Make little bullion leaves on either side of the stem.

SNOWDROPS

Work the stems and leaves in Whipped Backstitch using 2 strands of green embroidery thread. With white silk ribbon, make 3-5 Inverted Stab Stitches

down the side of the stem. Using 1 strand of green embroidery thread, work an upside-down Fly Stitch attached to the stem over the top of the snow-drop. Work 3 little Stab Stitches at the bottom of the snowdrop. On the other side of the stem, work Lazy Daisy Stitch (see diagram) using 1 strand of green embroidery thread.

TULIPS

Bring the ribbon up through the fabric at the top of the middle petal of the tulip. Make an Inverted Stab Stitch. Make two Inverted Stab Stitches, one on the right and one on the left of the middle petal, leaving a small space at the top, but inverting into the same hole at the bottom. Work the stems and leaves in two strands of green embroidery thread in Stem Stitch, and work a Fly Stitch at the base of the petals.

VIOLETS

First work clusters of heart-shaped leaves in Buttonhole Stitch using 2 strands of green embroidery thread. The flowers are five Inverted Stab Stitches worked centre outwards – two petals pointing upwards and three pointing down in violet silk ribbon. Make the centres of the flowers by working a French Knot in each, using 2 strands of yellow embroidery thread. The stems of the buds are worked in Stem Stitch using 2 strands of green embroidery thread. To make buds at the top of the stems, work a Fly Stitch using 2 strands of green embroidery thread and using violet silk ribbon, work a Lazy Daisy Stitch in the middle of the Fly Stitch.

6
SATIN RIBBON FLOWERS

IMPORTANT POINTS FOR SATIN RIBBON FLOWER

1. Choose a soft, satin ribbon, as it is easier on the fingers when you are making roses.

2. Remember, these flowers are prominent on the fabric – the wider the ribbon, the larger the flower.

3. Always use thread that matches the ribbon. The best needle to use is a No. 7 or 8 straw needle, and 2 strands of matching embroidery thread, as it does not knot or tangle.

4. Have a lighter or candle on hand to melt the ends of the satin ribbon; it stops it from fraying and makes it very washable.

SATIN RIBBON FLOWERS
Concertina Rose

This rose works particularly well on the narrower ribbon (8-10 mm width). Cut a length of ribbon 26mm and fold it at a right angle in the centre as per diagram A. Whichever ribbon is on the top, gets folded back first (diagram B). Then fold the other ribbon back. Keep on folding each alternative ribbon back – the fold will take on a square look. When the ribbon is used up, grasp the two ends and let go of the folded ribbon, which will spring up. Pull down gently on one ribbon – it doesn't matter which one – until the rose is formed. Do not pull too hard, otherwise you will lose the rose.

Stitch the rose from the base through the centre 3 or 4 times to secure it. Cut the ribbon off as close to the base as you can and seal it with the blue of the flame.

Attach onto your background fabric with matching thread, sewing between the folds, 6-7 times.

Double Ribbon Rose

Using 14mm width ribbon, cut a length of 22cm. For larger roses, use wider ribbon and cut it longer; for small roses, do the opposite. With shiny sides facing, melt the two raw ends together with a flame and push together using quick movements with the thumb and index finger (diagram A). It will fuse together nicely; be careful not to burn yourself. Turn the ribbon loop so the shiny side is outside and roll 3 times to make a tube with the double ribbon. Sew a few stitches into the middle of the tube.

Take the thread to the back of the tube, and fold the ribbon backwards and sew; repeat again and again, until you have finished your ribbon. Stitch your final fold under the rose. The Double Ribbon Rose is a chunkier rose, and is all shiny. If there is a little tail underneath the rose, cut it off and seal with a flame. It is now ready to attach. Attach onto your background fabric with matching thread, sewing between the folds 6 or 7 times.

Two-Tone Rose

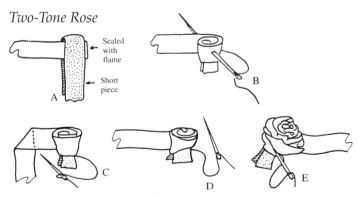

Cut a short piece of ribbon, about the length of your index finger. Seal the ribbon length end with the blue of the flame, and fold the short piece over the end of this (diagram A). Roll it tightly (4 or 5 times) to make a tube. Sew through the middle a few times to hold, so it doesn't unroll, and take the thread to the back of the tube (diagram B). With the tube in the right hand, fold the ribbon backwards with your left hand. Sew the fold down with a couple of stitches. Repeat this over and over – fold backwards and sew, until your rose is the desired size and shape. The ribbon will keep alternating shiny/matt, shiny/matt – hence the name "two-tone rose".

Cut the ribbon and seal the end with the blue of the flame. Stitch the final fold under the rose. Cut off any of the short piece of ribbon, close to the base, and seal with the flame under the rose. It is now ready to attach onto your background fabric. Attach with matching thread, sewing between the folds 6 or 7 times.

"Victorian" Rose

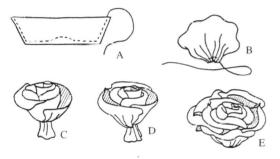

For the Victorian roses, you can either use wide satin ribbon (20 30 mm width) or the moiré taffeta (25 mm width) ribbon. The centre of the rose is made the same as the "two-tone" rose, only fold back 5 or 6 times before ending off. The rest of the petals are made separately using a trapezoid shape. Cut 5 to 6 trapezoid shapes – the bottom being 8cm in length. Please note that if you are using the satin ribbon, you must seal the sides of your trapezoid with a flame – it is unnecessary with the moiré taffeta ribbon.

Make small running stitches along the sides and bottom lifting the stitching up slightly in the middle (diagram A). Pull the thread so it gathers up and stitch each petal individually around the centre of the rose, working clockwise and overlapping each petal, shiny side facing the centre. Add as many

petals as you need for the size of the rose you require. Cut the tail off at the bottom, seal with a flame, and it is ready to be attached. Attach onto your background fabric with matching thread, sewing between the folds 6 or 7 times.

Ribbon Rosebuds
The rosebuds can be done with either the "two-tone" or "double ribbon" rose method. Just make your tube, turn the ribbon backwards 2 or 3 times, sew and end off.

1. Gathered Leaf

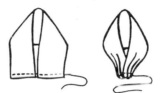

The width of the ribbon can vary from 8 to 14mm. Cut a piece of ribbon about 8cm in length and seal the raw edges with a flame. Fold the ribbon into an arrow shape and make a small running stitch along the wide edge. Pull the thread to gather – and stitch it firmly onto background fabric, tucking the raw edges under the rose.

2. Fold Over Leaf

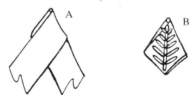

Cut a rectangle of ribbon 7cm in length – seal both raw edges with a flame. Fold the top corners with the right hand side going over the left – diagram A). Turn the raw edges back and stitch at the back of the leaf.

Attach the leaf to the background fabric, either with invisible stitching around the leaf or else do an Extended Fly Stitch down the centre of the leaf in 2 strands of green embroidery thread.

7
PROJECTS

split stitch
embroidery
thread
2 strands

ANNIVERSARY HEART

Work all your flowers using the combination
stitches for silk ribbon flowers. Work your
embroidery next and fill in any gaps with Colonial
Knots in silk ribbon.

The monograms, angels and inscription are
optional. It was made by Olga for her husband
Fernando for their wedding anniversary.

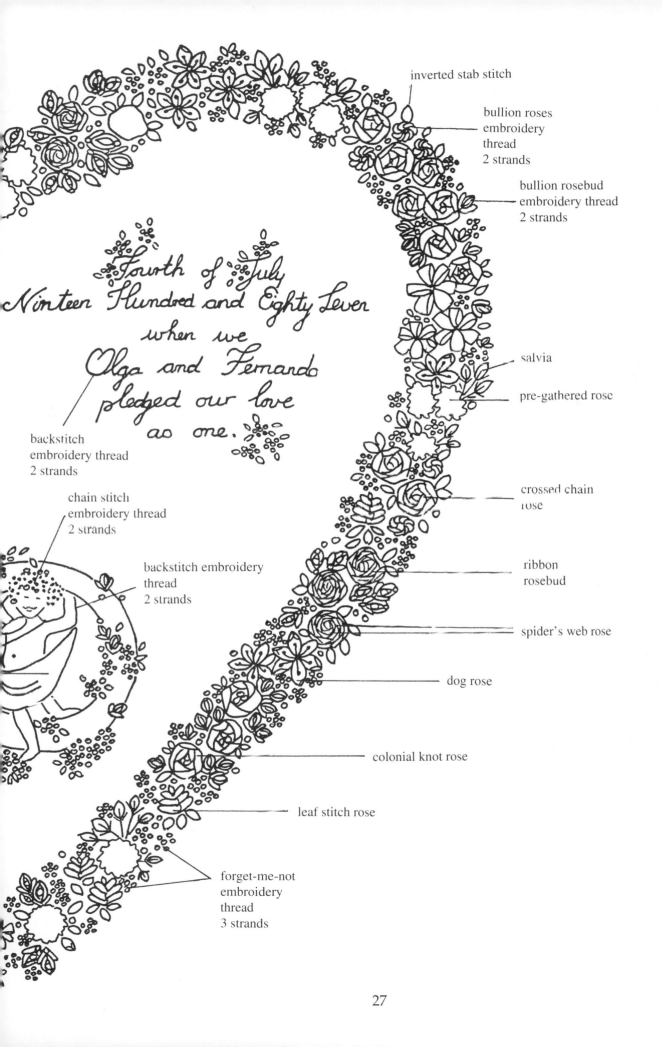

inverted stab stitch

bullion roses
embroidery
thread
2 strands

bullion rosebud
embroidery thread
2 strands

Fourth of July
Ninteen Hundred and Eighty Leven
when we
Olga and Fernando
pledged our love
as one.

salvia

pre-gathered rose

backstitch
embroidery thread
2 strands

chain stitch
embroidery thread
2 strands

backstitch embroidery
thread
2 strands

crossed chain
rose

ribbon
rosebud

spider's web rose

dog rose

colonial knot rose

leaf stitch rose

forget-me-not
embroidery
thread
3 strands

COUNTRY GARDEN CUSHIONS (SALLI VAN RENSBURG)

This is a charming array of flowers, worked in a combination of silk ribbon and embroidery thread. Draw a block 21cm x 21cm, and divide it into 7cm squares. Into each square, referring to Chapter 5 as a guideline, work your choice of flowers, or choose all the different roses.

This design is wonderful for cushions, or framed as a picture. It also looks good worked in individual bunches of flowers on garments.

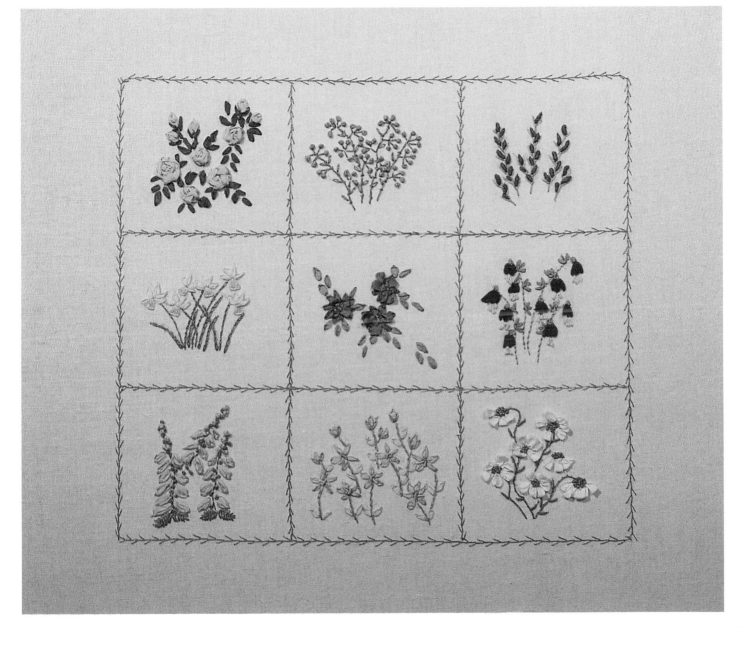

ANTIQUE HANDKERCHIEFS (ANNE NICOLSON)

Both these handkerchiefs are of great sentimental value, as they belonged to Anne's grandmother. First, trace the design onto your handkerchief. Then tack it well, from the centre out, onto a background fabric of your choice. Work your silk ribbon flowers first, and then all your embroidery stitches. The bows are optional – they were used to cover old stains that could not be removed. Embroider little pockets of flowers around the handkerchief and into any lace work. Work either Feather Stitch and French Knots around the edges of the handkerchief or Chain Stitch in one strand of thread. This is to secure the handkerchief for stretching and framing purposes.

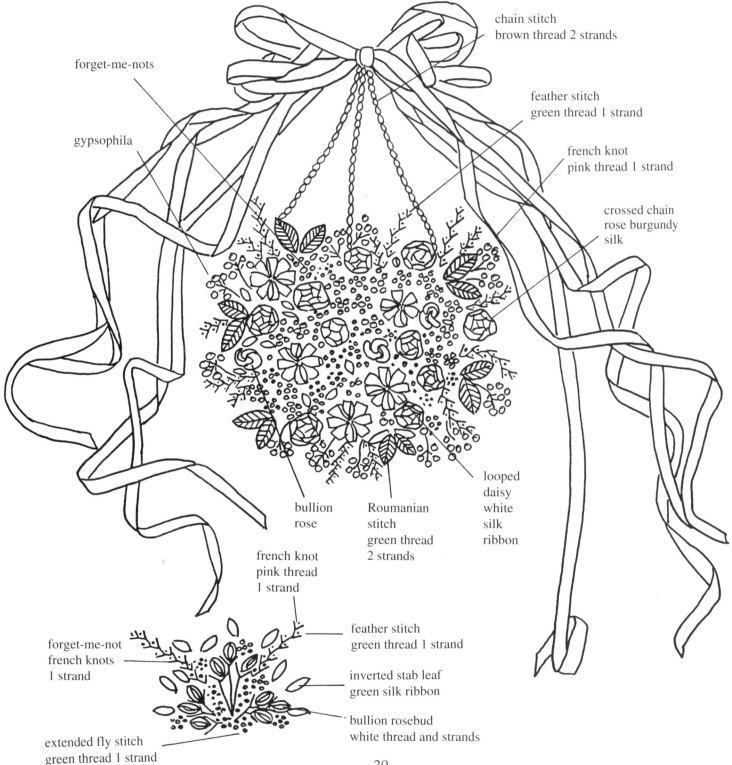

forget-me-nots

gypsophila

chain stitch
brown thread 2 strands

feather stitch
green thread 1 strand

french knot
pink thread 1 strand

crossed chain
rose burgundy
silk

bullion
rose

french knot
pink thread
1 strand

Roumanian
stitch
green thread
2 strands

looped
daisy
white
silk
ribbon

forget-me-not
french knots
1 strand

feather stitch
green thread 1 strand

inverted stab leaf
green silk ribbon

bullion rosebud
white thread and strands

extended fly stitch
green thread 1 strand

30

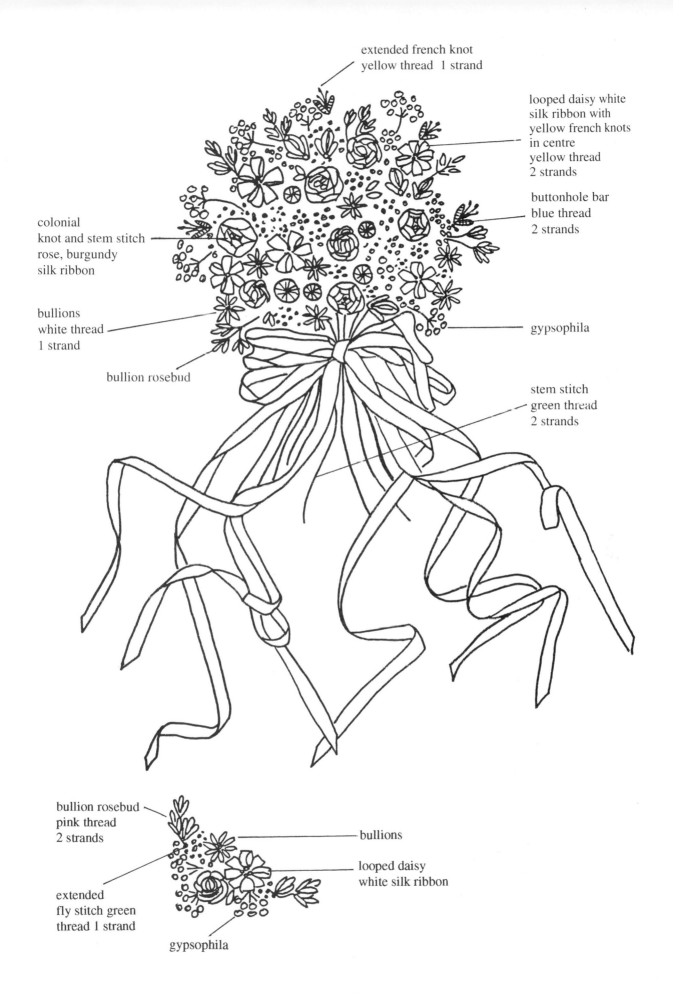

extended french knot
yellow thread 1 strand

looped daisy white
silk ribbon with
yellow french knots
in centre
yellow thread
2 strands

buttonhole bar
blue thread
2 strands

colonial
knot and stem stitch
rose, burgundy
silk ribbon

bullions
white thread
1 strand

bullion rosebud

gypsophila

stem stitch
green thread
2 strands

bullion rosebud
pink thread
2 strands

bullions

looped daisy
white silk ribbon

extended
fly stitch green
thread 1 strand

gypsophila

BUTTERFLY SHIRT (ROBIN BARNETT)

Have fun "jazzing up" an old shirt or blouse. Work your silk ribbon stitches, followed by your embroidery stitches.

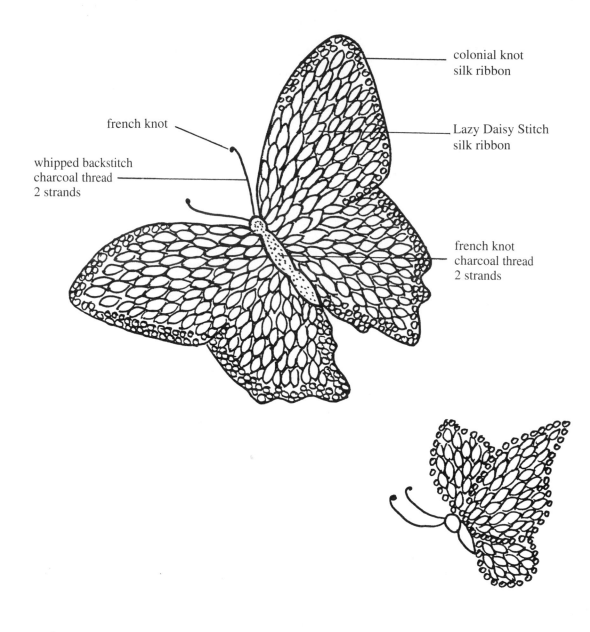

colonial knot
silk ribbon

Lazy Daisy Stitch
silk ribbon

french knot

whipped backstitch
charcoal thread
2 strands

french knot
charcoal thread
2 strands

ELEGANT TOWELS (SALLI VAN RENSBURG)

A touch of silk and satin ribbon on towels makes a wonderful gift, or can enhance one's own bathroom (see diagram for instructions).

The "double ribbon" rose is best for use on towels, as they withstand vigorous washing.

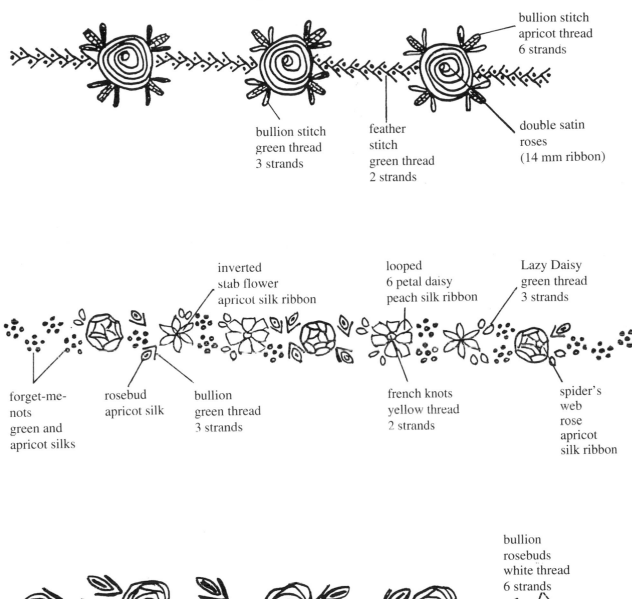

bullion stitch
apricot thread
6 strands

bullion stitch
green thread
3 strands

feather
stitch
green thread
2 strands

double satin
roses
(14 mm ribbon)

inverted
stab flower
apricot silk ribbon

looped
6 petal daisy
peach silk ribbon

Lazy Daisy
green thread
3 strands

forget-me-
nots
green and
apricot silks

rosebud
apricot silk

bullion
green thread
3 strands

french knots
yellow thread
2 strands

spider's
web
rose
apricot
silk ribbon

bullion
rosebuds
white thread
6 strands

double satin
ribbon rose
(14 mm ribbon)

bullion
stitch
green thread
3 strands

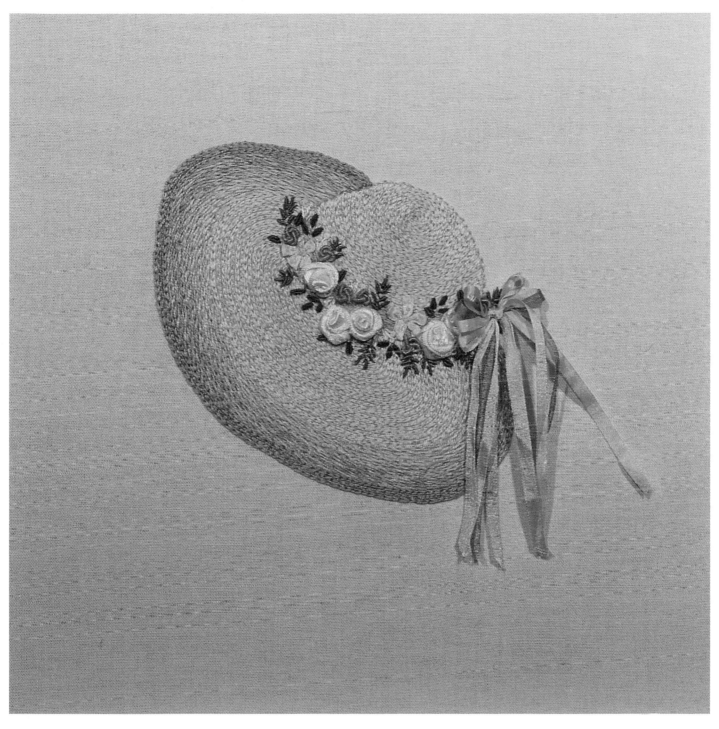

EMBROIDERED HAT (JENNY CLAY)

Choose 2 shades of wheat-coloured thread for the hat. Work four rows of Chain Stitch around the brim of the hat using 2 strands of the darkest colour thread. Next, work 8 rows of Stem Stitch using 1 strand of each colour thread on the same needle. The rest of the hat brim and crown is worked in Chain Stitch using 2 strands of the lighter shade of thread.

Work your "two-tone" roses with 8mm white satin ribbon and attach. Work your embroidery stitches and silk ribbon next, and make a bow with any left-over silk ribbon.

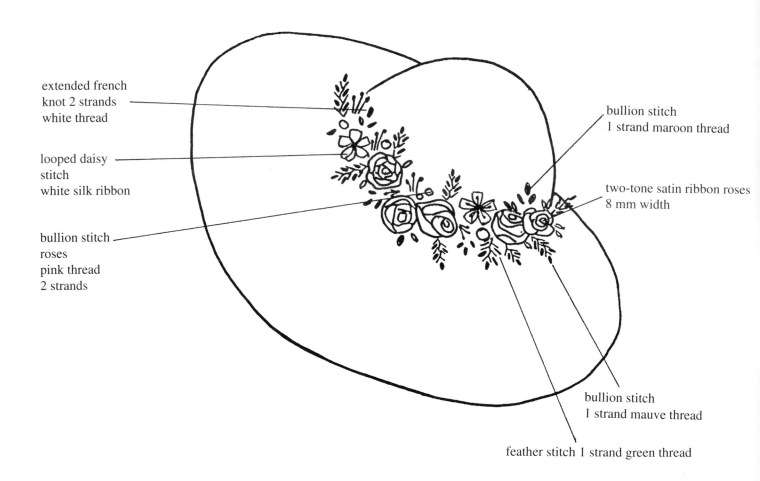

extended french
knot 2 strands
white thread

looped daisy
stitch
white silk ribbon

bullion stitch
roses
pink thread
2 strands

bullion stitch
1 strand maroon thread

two-tone satin ribbon roses
8 mm width

bullion stitch
1 strand mauve thread

feather stitch 1 strand green thread

ENCHANTING KNITWEAR

Add some colour, style and panache to your wardrobe with some silk and satin ribbon embroidery.

You can have such fun, giving your clothing a new individual look at very little expense.

Black jersey   (LYN COOMBES)

Work a large Feather Stitch using six strands of black embroidery thread around the neckline of the jersey. Make a secure beginning with a knot and a Backstitch on the inside. This makes the washing process easier. Make the required number of "two-tone" roses in 10mm red satin ribbon. Put them aside to be attached last. Work your gypsophila, red silk ribbon, rosebuds and silver Lazy Daisy leaves. Then attach your satin roses.

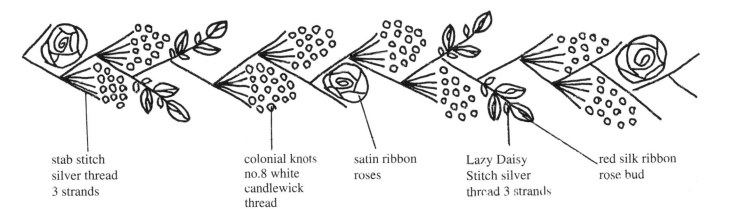

stab stitch
silver thread
3 strands

colonial knots
no.8 white
candlewick
thread

satin ribbon
roses

Lazy Daisy
Stitch silver
thread 3 strands

red silk ribbon
rose bud

Dusty pink jersey (LYN COOMBES)
Work your stems first, in either 6 strands of green embroidery thread or a fine
tapestry wool. There is no particular order in which the stitches should be done.
Just work at random and have fun. Finish with the bullion butterflies on
the shoulder.

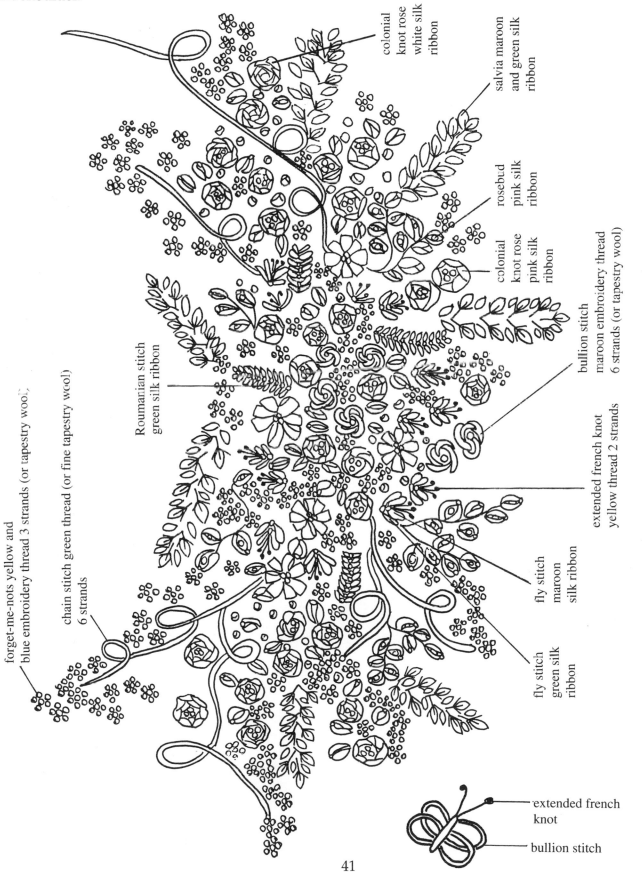

colonial
knot rose
white silk
ribbon

salvia maroon
and green silk
ribbon

rosebud
pink silk
ribbon

colonial
knot rose
pink silk
ribbon

bullion stitch
maroon embroidery thread
6 strands (or tapestry wool)

Roumanian stitch
green silk ribbon

extended french knot
yellow thread 2 strands

fly stitch
maroon
silk ribbon

forget-me-nots yellow and
blue embroidery thread 3 strands (or tapestry wool)

chain stitch green thread (or fine tapestry wool)
6 strands

fly stitch
green silk
ribbon

extended french
knot

bullion stitch

41

GREEN JERSEY

DUSTY PINK JERSEY

Lavender jersey (LYN COOMBES)
Work the stems of the lavender
first. Then work your flowers
with silk ribbon, using your
left-over ribbon to tie a bow
and stitch it onto the stems.

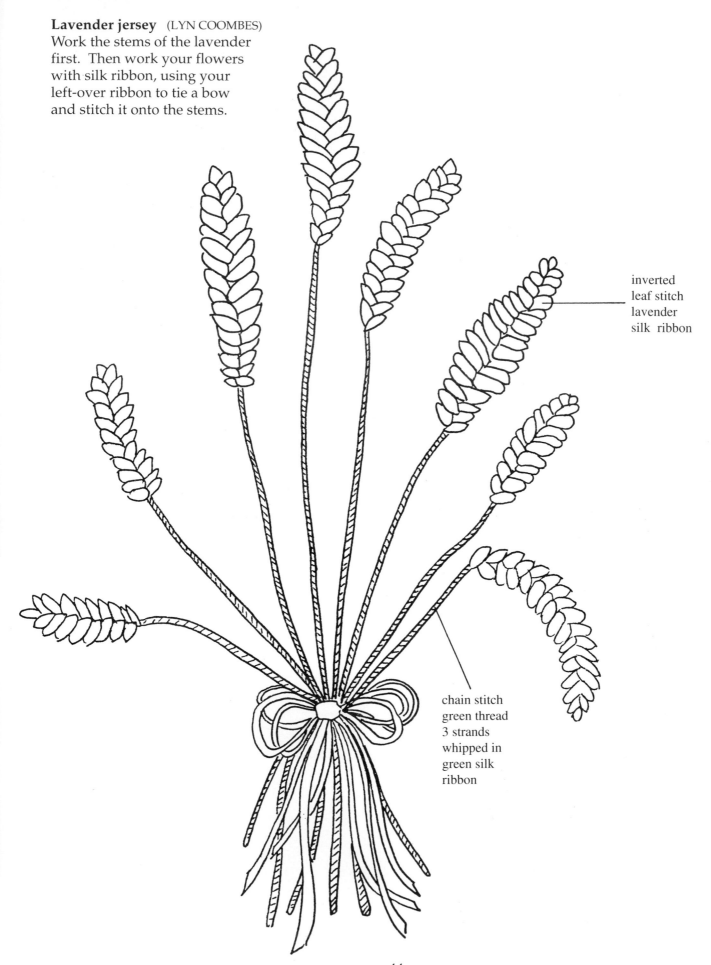

inverted
leaf stitch
lavender
silk ribbon

chain stitch
green thread
3 strands
whipped in
green silk
ribbon

Green jersey (SUE THERON)

Work thc neckline in Feather Stitch using green silk ribbon. If you battle to get your Feather Stitch even, take a tape measure or ruler and measure 2cm from the edge of the neckband and pin all the way around. Now run a tacking stitch around, using the pins as your guideline. Remove pins.

Work all your stitches into the "V" of the Feather Stitch. There is no particular order in which the stitches should be done, but it is easier to complete one particular stitch first, ie. all Colonial Knots, then all Lazy Daisies, etc ....

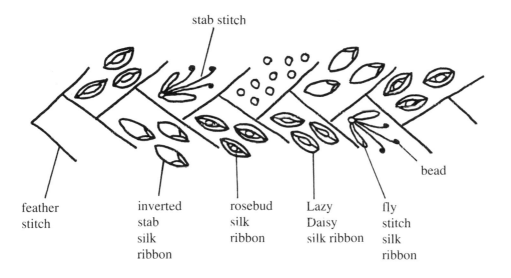

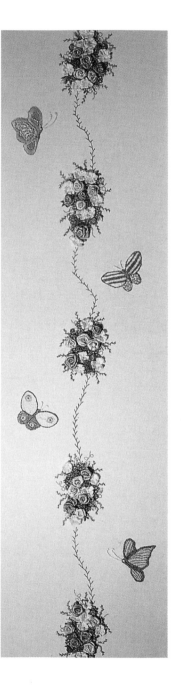

FLOWER POSY (DIANNE MOOLMAN)
WITH BUTTERFLIES

Make the required number of satin ribbon roses, using the "double satin" and "two-tone" ribbon rose technique. Put them aside to attach later.

You can have fun with the embroidered butterflies using colours of your choice. Work them first, together with the embroidery stitches on the posy. Work your looped daisies next, leaving the satin ribbon roses to be attached last.

french knot pink and white thread 2 strands

raised stem stitch dark pink thread 2 strands

raised stem stitch white thread 2 strands

chain stitch green 2 strands

buttonhole stitch pink thread 2 strands

extended french knot yellow thread 2 strands

french knot yellow thread 2 strands

french knots green thread 2 strands

outline the wings in chain stitch green thread

french knots green thread 2 strands

looped daisy white silk ribbon

french knots yellow thread 2 strands

satin roses

backstitch green thread 2 strands

whipped backstitch yellow thread 2 strands

feather stitch green thread 1 strand

french knot pink thread 1 strand

bullion stitch green thread 2 strands

french knot forget-me-not yellow centre blue around 2 strands

extended french knot yellow thread 2 strands

buttonhole bar stitch pink thread 2 strands

split stitch yellow 2 strands

french knots blue thread 2 strands

french knots dark pink thread 2 strands

buttonhole wheel light pink thread 2 strands

vertical spider's web pale mauve thread 2 strands

chain stitch dark pink thread 2 strands

satin stitch blue thread 2 strands

48

HAT BOXES (SALLI VAN RENSBURG) (ELSPETH KIRKMAN)

For the hat box, you will need: 630g cardboard (1m long), 0.5m fabric (for outside of box), 0.5m fabric for inside of box (preferably cotton), and 1.30m applique paper.

Draw on the cardboard and cut out 2 strips 4cm x 92cm (lid) and 19cm x 88cm (base). Draw on the cardboard and cut out 2 circles, (ie) :

28cm diameter – set a compass on 14cm and draw a circle
27cm diameter – set a compass on 13.5cm and draw a circle

METHOD:

1. Place cardboard templates onto the smooth side of the applique paper.

2. Draw with a soft 2B pencil around the templates, cut out with paper scissors.

3. Place rough side of the applique paper onto the wrong side of fabric for lining the inside of the box. Iron and cut out with pinking shears. Put aside.

4. Draw a second set on the applique paper, the size of your templates adding a seam allowance of 2cm and cut out.

5. Repeat for the outside fabric of the box. Cut out with ordinary scissors.

6. Peel the applique paper off the outside fabric and iron onto the template, with the seam allowance showing all the way around. Turn the seam allowance over the cardboard and iron down. Snip around the circles for an even fit.

7. Peel the applique paper off the inside fabric and iron onto the template, covering your seam allowance.

8. Gently wrap the base strip around the base circle and mark with a pencil. There must be an overlap. Glue together with a glue gun working quickly, and hold firmly for 1 minute. If you do not have a glue gun, use cold wood glue and peg top and bottom of your cylinders; it will take longer to set if cold glue is used.

9. Place the base circle inside the base cylinder ensuring a snug fit. Glue in place on the inside with cold wood glue.

10. For the lid, repeat steps 6 to 9.

Have fun decorating the hat box lid with satin or moiré taffeta ribbon roses, silk bows, braiding, cording, etc.

4cm x 92cm   LID

27cm DIAMETER BASE

19cm x 88cm   BASE

28cm DIAMETER BASE

Comfrey

HERBS

Comfrey (NASREEN THOKAN)

Trace the leaves out first onto applique paper – rough side up – cut out. Iron the paper rough side down onto wrong side of fabric. Cut out and peel off the paper. Place the leaves into position and iron on. Work your embroidery stitches onto the leaves first, then work your ribbon stems and flowers.

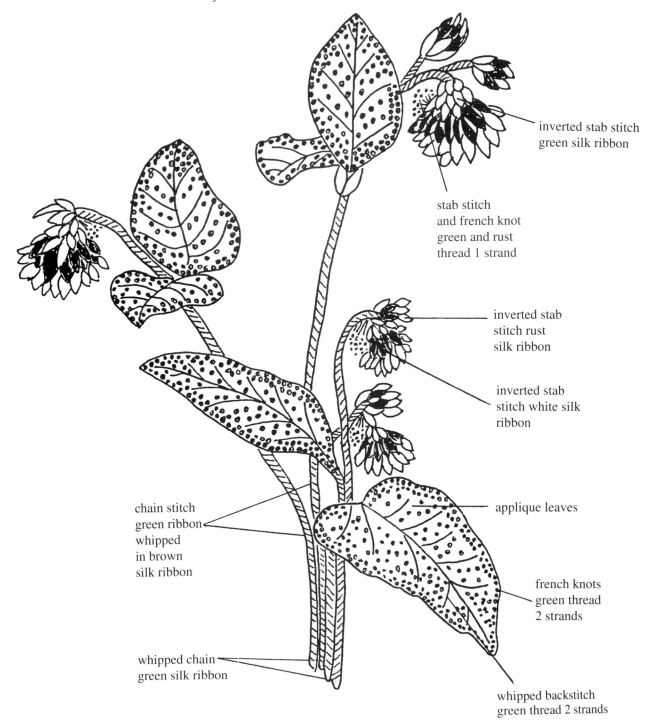

inverted stab stitch
green silk ribbon

stab stitch
and french knot
green and rust
thread 1 strand

inverted stab
stitch rust
silk ribbon

inverted stab
stitch white silk
ribbon

applique leaves

chain stitch
green ribbon
whipped
in brown
silk ribbon

french knots
green thread
2 strands

whipped chain
green silk ribbon

whipped backstitch
green thread 2 strands

52

Rue (NASREEN THOKAN)
Work your stems and leaves first, followed by your flowers.

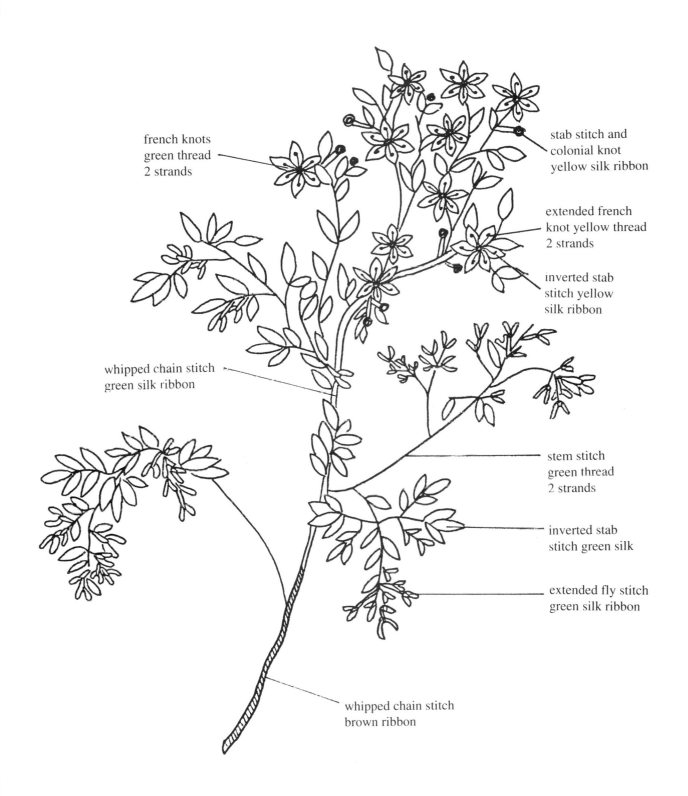

french knots
green thread
2 strands

stab stitch and
colonial knot
yellow silk ribbon

extended french
knot yellow thread
2 strands

inverted stab
stitch yellow
silk ribbon

whipped chain stitch
green silk ribbon

stem stitch
green thread
2 strands

inverted stab
stitch green silk

extended fly stitch
green silk ribbon

whipped chain stitch
brown ribbon

SMOCKED DRESS (JOYCE DE VAAL)
Add a few satin ribbon roses onto smocked clothing for a bit of fun.

Sage (NASREEN THOKAN)
Work your stems and leaves first, followed by your flowers.
   The inside borders are worked in Feather Stitch and the outside border is a
Backstitch with Bullions and French Knots.

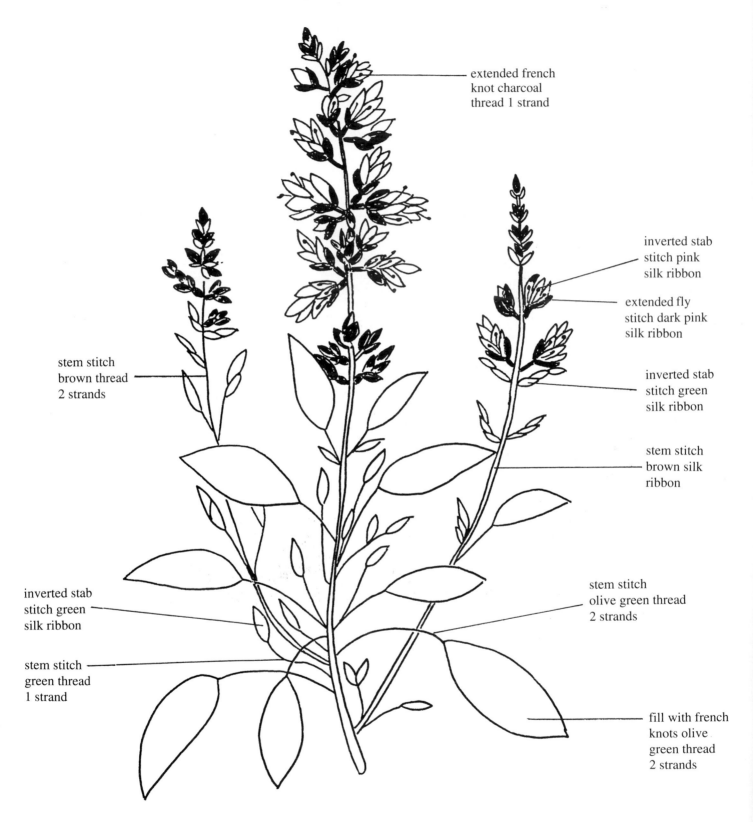

extended french
knot charcoal
thread 1 strand

inverted stab
stitch pink
silk ribbon

extended fly
stitch dark pink
silk ribbon

stem stitch
brown thread
2 strands

inverted stab
stitch green
silk ribbon

stem stitch
brown silk
ribbon

inverted stab
stitch green
silk ribbon

stem stitch
green thread
1 strand

stem stitch
olive green thread
2 strands

fill with french
knots olive
green thread
2 strands

KALEIDOSCOPE OF COLOUR BOUQUET (NASREEN THOKAN)

This is a beautiful piece of work, using left-over pieces of ribbon. Work your embroidery stitches and stems first, then make all your satin ribbon roses. They are a combination of the "concertina" rose, "two-tone" rose and "double satin" rose. Put aside.

Make your looped daisies, and attach all your roses. Take your green silk ribbon last and work your Loop Stitch in between all your roses and your Inverted Stabs around the outer edge.

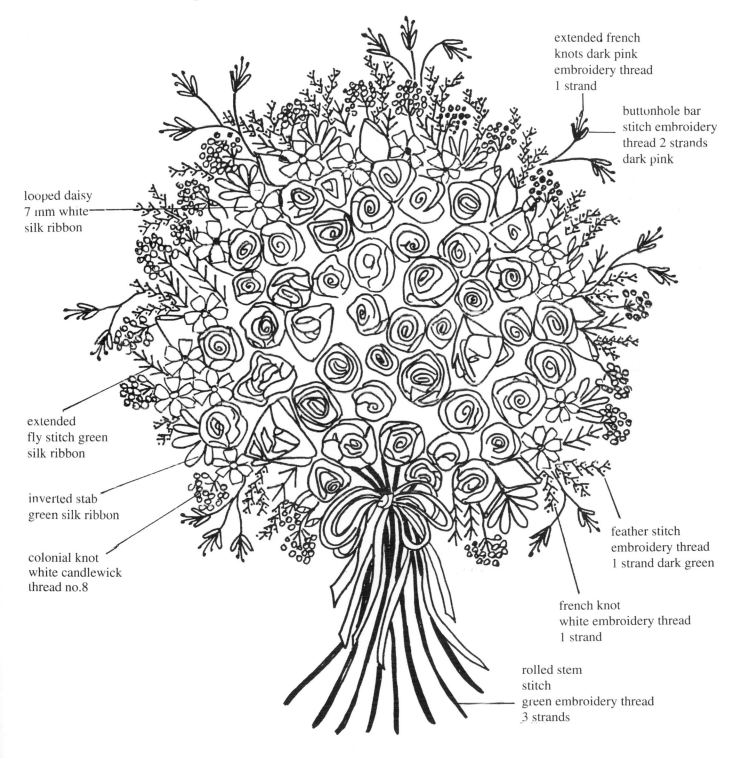

extended french
knots dark pink
embroidery thread
1 strand

buttonhole bar
stitch embroidery
thread 2 strands
dark pink

looped daisy
7 mm white
silk ribbon

extended
fly stitch green
silk ribbon

inverted stab
green silk ribbon

colonial knot
white candlewick
thread no.8

feather stitch
embroidery thread
1 strand dark green

french knot
white embroidery thread
1 strand

rolled stem
stitch
green embroidery thread
3 strands

57

OLD WORLD GARDEN CLOCK (FAY SCHERER)

Work all your flowers using the combination stitches for silk ribbon flowers. When all your flowers are complete, take two strands of green embroidery thread and fill in with French Knots and Extended French Knots in any gaps between the base of the flowers. Complete the circle with a Feather Stitch around the outside edge using 2 strands of green embroidery thread. With gold thread, work a Colonial Knot in every "V".

Refer to the Oval Spring Flower Clock for assembly.

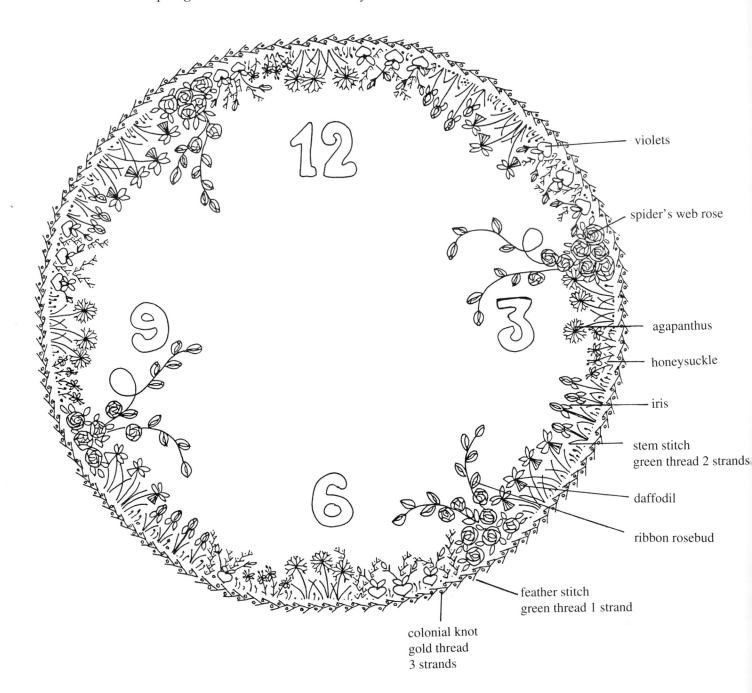

violets

spider's web rose

agapanthus

honeysuckle

iris

stem stitch
green thread 2 strands

daffodil

ribbon rosebud

feather stitch
green thread 1 strand

colonial knot
gold thread
3 strands

OLD WORLD ROSE CLOCK (LYN COOMBES)

Work your stems first in embroidery thread. Next, work all your different silk ribbon roses and leaves – refer to Chapter 5, Combination Stitches for Silk Ribbon Flowers. Work your gypsophila and border next, followed by your Roman numerals.

Refer to the Oval Spring Flower Clock for completion.

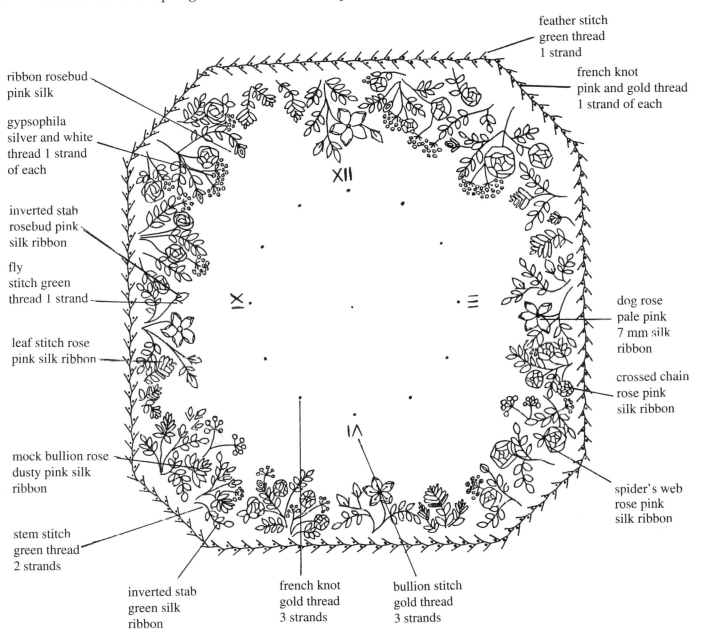

feather stitch
green thread
1 strand

french knot
pink and gold thread
1 strand of each

ribbon rosebud
pink silk

gypsophila
silver and white
thread 1 strand
of each

inverted stab
rosebud pink
silk ribbon

fly
stitch green
thread 1 strand

leaf stitch rose
pink silk ribbon

mock bullion rose
dusty pink silk
ribbon

stem stitch
green thread
2 strands

dog rose
pale pink
7 mm silk
ribbon

crossed chain
rose pink
silk ribbon

spider's web
rose pink
silk ribbon

inverted stab
green silk
ribbon

french knot
gold thread
3 strands

bullion stitch
gold thread
3 strands

OVAL SPRING FLOWER CLOCK (LYN COOMBES)

Work all your flowers using the Combination Stitches for Silk Ribbon Flowers. The clock numbers are worked in one strand of embroidery thread using your Basic Crewel Stitches in Chapter 4.

Once your clock is complete and stretched onto a board, mark your centre point. Cut a tiny cross through the fabric and muslin, and carefully drill a hole through the board. Attach your clock mechanism.

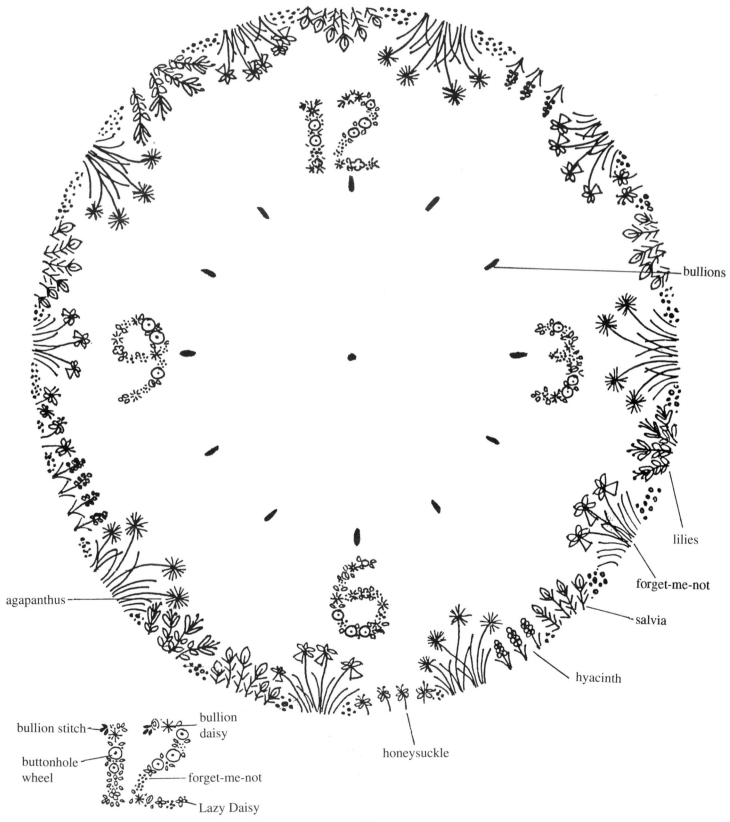

bullions

lilies

forget-me-not

salvia

hyacinth

agapanthus

honeysuckle

bullion stitch

bullion daisy

buttonhole wheel

forget-me-not

Lazy Daisy

OVAL SUMMER GARDEN CLOCK   (SALLI VAN RENSBURG)

Work all your flowers using the Combination Stitches for Silk Ribbon Flowers.
When all your flowers are complete, take two strands of green embroidery
thread and fill in with French Knots in any gaps between the base of the flowers.
It will give you a more defined circle. The numbers are worked in one strand of
embroidery thread, simply using various greens.
   Refer to the Oval Spring Flower Clock for instructions on how to complete.

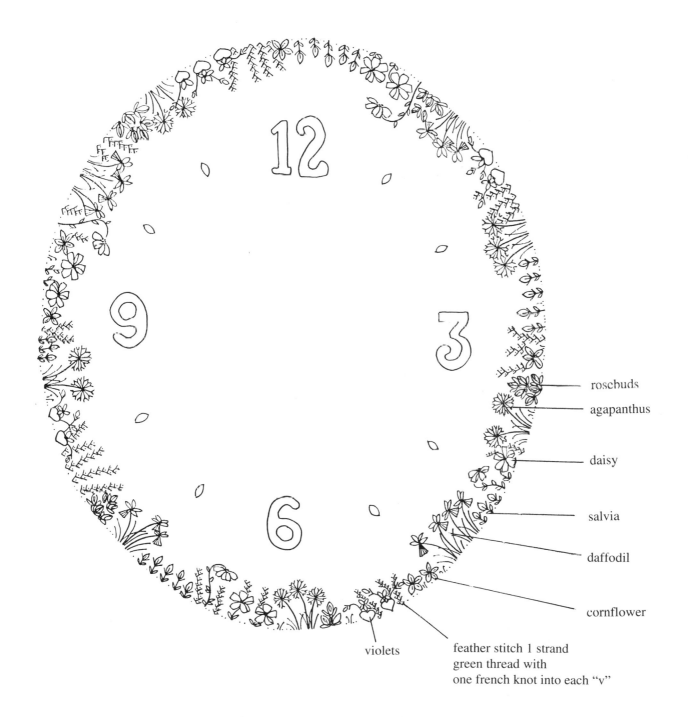

rosebuds
agapanthus
daisy
salvia
daffodil
cornflower
violets
feather stitch 1 strand
green thread with
one french knot into each "v"

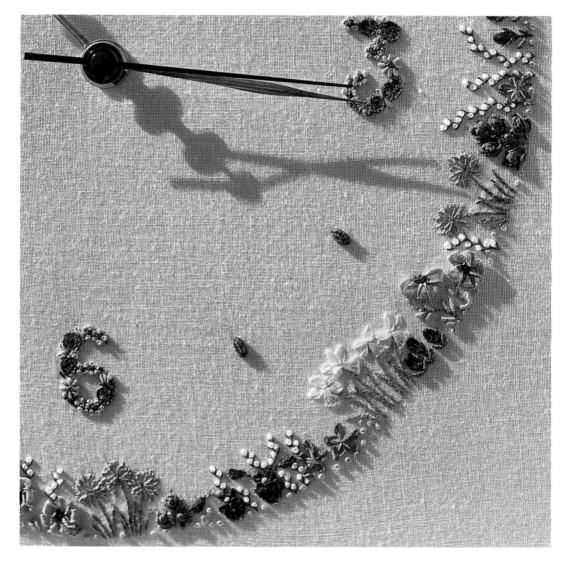

OVAL OF YELLOW ROSES (EVA COCK)

Work the stems, leaves, bullion rosebuds and Feather Stitch first. Make the required number of satin ribbon roses using 14mm width ribbon using the "double ribbon" and "two-one" techniques and attach them into place. With a left-over piece of satin ribbon, make a bow and attach it on with a little forget-me-not flower in 3 strands of embroidery thread.

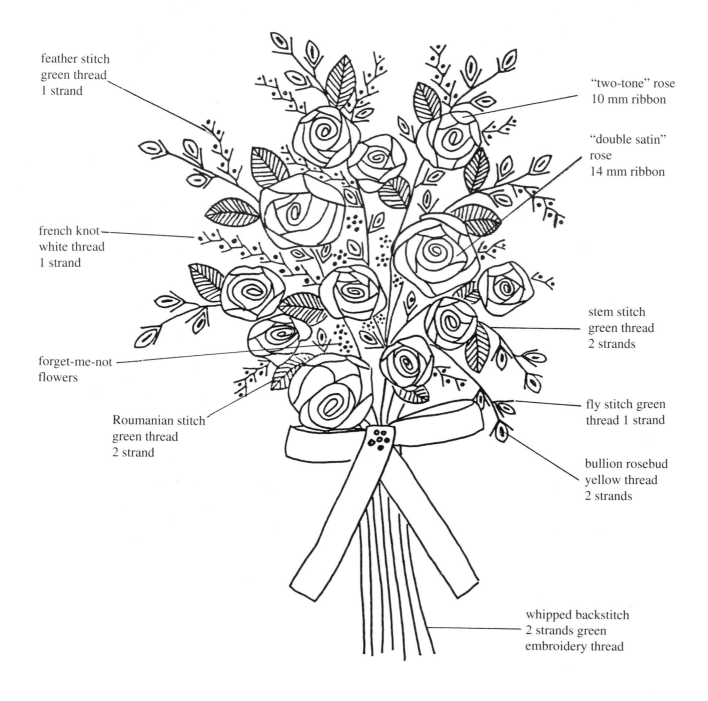

feather stitch
green thread
1 strand

"two-tone" rose
10 mm ribbon

"double satin"
rose
14 mm ribbon

french knot
white thread
1 strand

stem stitch
green thread
2 strands

forget-me-not
flowers

fly stitch green
thread 1 strand

Roumanian stitch
green thread
2 strand

bullion rosebud
yellow thread
2 strands

whipped backstitch
2 strands green
embroidery thread

OVAL OF PINK ROSES (EVA COCK)

Work the bow, stems, leaves and koeksister roses first, then work your looped silk ribbon daisies. Make the required number of satin ribbon roses out of 14mm ribbon using the two-tone ribbon technique, and attach into place.

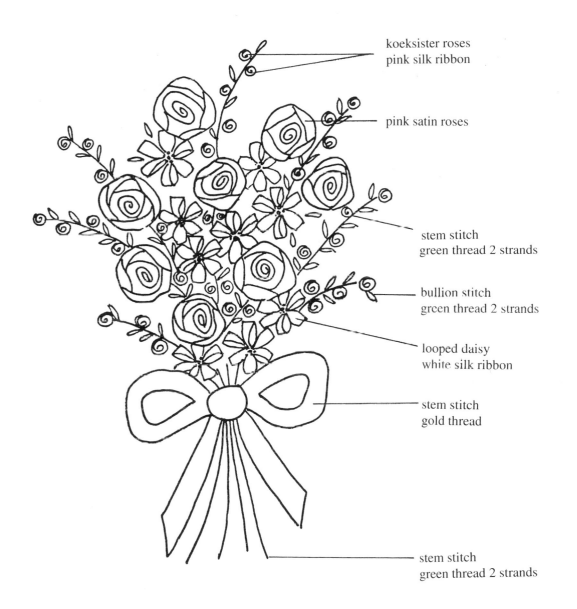

koeksister roses
pink silk ribbon

pink satin roses

stem stitch
green thread 2 strands

bullion stitch
green thread 2 strands

looped daisy
white silk ribbon

stem stitch
gold thread

stem stitch
green thread 2 strands

PAINTED BENCH (SUE HAMMILL)

With a permanent black fineliner pen, outline the bench and hat. Test your paint on a scrap piece of fabric first, to get the feel of your brush. Dilute the paint with water, and after each colour change, iron the paintwork to seal it onto the fabric. Use only fabric or stencil paint. Tack your muslin behind and begin with your silk ribbon and embroidery stitches, studying the labelled sketch.

inverted stab leaves
green silk ribbon

looped daisy
yellow silk ribbon

salvia

chain stitch
brown thread
2 strands

raised stem
coral thread
2 strands

buttonhole stitch
mauve thread
2 strands

Roumanian
stitch green
thread
2 strands

violets

honey suckle

forget-me-nots

buttonhole
wheel
white thread
1 strand

lavender

colonial knot
and stem stitch
rose

inverted
stab leaf
green silk ribbon

whipped
backstitch
green thread
2 strands

POPPY AND DAISY FIELD (SALLI VAN RENSBURG)

For the painting, refer to the Painted Bench.

Work your stems and embroidery stitches first, followed by the white silk ribbon daisies.

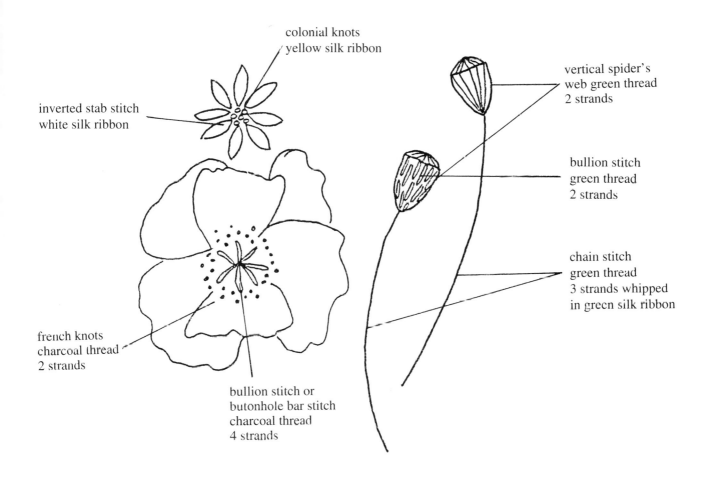

colonial knots
yellow silk ribbon

vertical spider's
web green thread
2 strands

inverted stab stitch
white silk ribbon

bullion stitch
green thread
2 strands

chain stitch
green thread
3 strands whipped
in green silk ribbon

french knots
charcoal thread
2 strands

bullion stitch or
butonhole bar stitch
charcoal thread
4 strands

SPRING HEART CUSHION (SALLI VAN RENSBURG)

Work your silk ribbon roses and daisies first, remembering to keep your ribbon loose on the roses, as it looks more natural.

Next, work all your other ribbon flowers, followed by your greenery and embroidery, fill in the empty spaces with colonial knots.

An economical way to save ribbon is to move to the next flower by making Colonial Knots (1cm apart) in between.

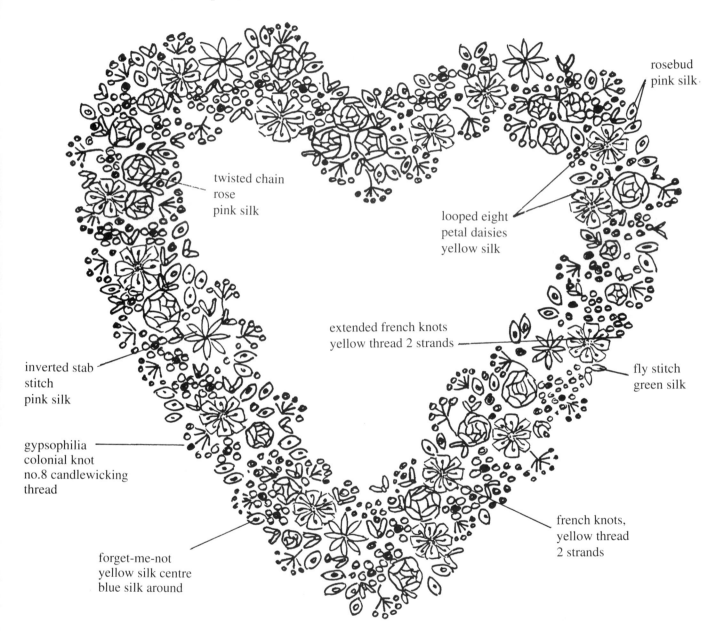

rosebud
pink silk

twisted chain
rose
pink silk

looped eight
petal daisies
yellow silk

extended french knots
yellow thread 2 strands

fly stitch
green silk

inverted stab
stitch
pink silk

gypsophilia
colonial knot
no.8 candlewicking
thread

french knots,
yellow thread
2 strands

forget-me-not
yellow silk centre
blue silk around

76

BOW ENHANCED WITH FLOWERS (SALLI VAN RENSBURG)

Work your bow first in Raised Stem, as a lot of the stems and flowers are worked over it. The stems will be worked next, followed by the roses, salvia, buds and leaves.

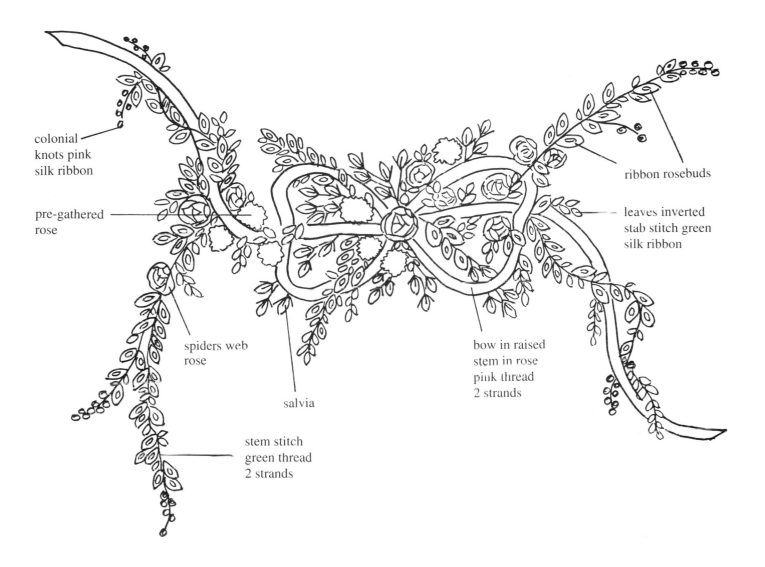

colonial knots pink silk ribbon

pre-gathered rose

spiders web rose

salvia

stem stitch green thread 2 strands

bow in raised stem in rose pink thread 2 strands

ribbon rosebuds

leaves inverted stab stitch green silk ribbon

VICTORIAN PINK ROSE CUSHION

BOW ENHANCED WITH FLOWERS

VICTORIAN PINK ROSE CUSHION (CHERYL WRIGHT)
Work the embroidery stitches first. Next work your silk ribbon leaves and stem.
Make the "Victorian" roses and buds and attach last.

bullion stitch rosebud
dusty pink thread 6 strands

back stitch green thread 2 strands

Roumanian stitch
green thread
3 strands

inverted leaf stitch
green silk ribbon

whipped chain stitch
green silk ribbon

"Victorian" rose
dusty pink moiré
taffeta ribbon

rosebud
dusty pink moiré
taffeta ribbon

VICTORIAN ROSES AND JASMINE ARRANGEMENT (RENÉ WALKER)
Work the copper jug first in your embroidery thread. Remember to keep your hoop taut, especially with your long Stab Stitches which shadow the jug.

   Work your silk leaves and gypsophila next, followed by your rosebuds and jasmine. The roses are made using the "Victorian" rose technique with moiré taffeta ribbon and are attached last.

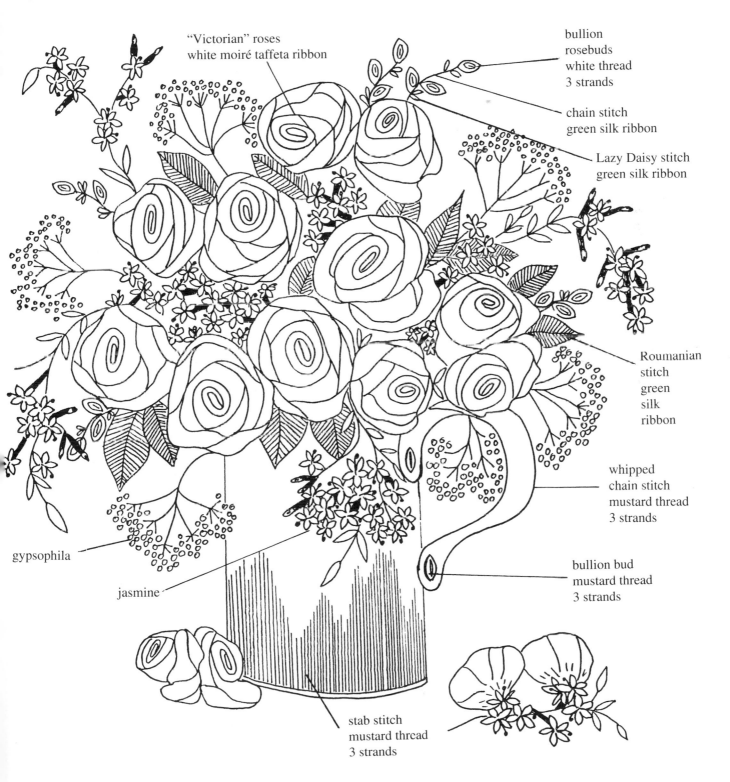

"Victorian" roses
white moiré taffeta ribbon

bullion
rosebuds
white thread
3 strands

chain stitch
green silk ribbon

Lazy Daisy stitch
green silk ribbon

Roumanian
stitch
green
silk
ribbon

whipped
chain stitch
mustard thread
3 strands

bullion bud
mustard thread
3 strands

gypsophila

jasmine

stab stitch
mustard thread
3 strands

WHITE VICTORIAN ROSES (BARBARA KAMPS)

Work your Victorian roses first with the 25mm satin ribbon. Put aside. Work your stems and leaves next in embroidery thread, followed by your gypsophila. Attach your Victorian roses. Make your satin ribbon leaves and attach with Extended Fly Stitch, tucking the ends of the leaves underneath the roses.

   This particular project has great sentimental value. The background fabric was a piece left over from the bridesmaid's dress, and the satin ribbon was originally tied to the bridal car.

"Victorian" roses
white satin
25 mm ribbon

Roumanian stitch
green thread
3 strands

colonial knot
no.8 white
candlewick thread

backstitch
green thread
2 strands

green satin
leaves (10 mm
width ribbon)
secured onto
fabric with
extended fly
stitch green
thread
2 strands

stem stitch
green thread
3 strands

84

VICTORIAN ROSE BOUQUET (SALLI VAN RENSBURG)

This piece of work, which has an old world charm, has been worked with moiré taffeta ribbon. Make the "Victorian" roses first and put them aside. Then work your stems, rosebuds and Feather Stitch in embroidery thread. Stitch your roses into place. Make your satin ribbon leaves, tucking the ends under the roses and blind hem them into place with matching thread.

Tie a bow with pieces of silk ribbon and stitch onto stems.

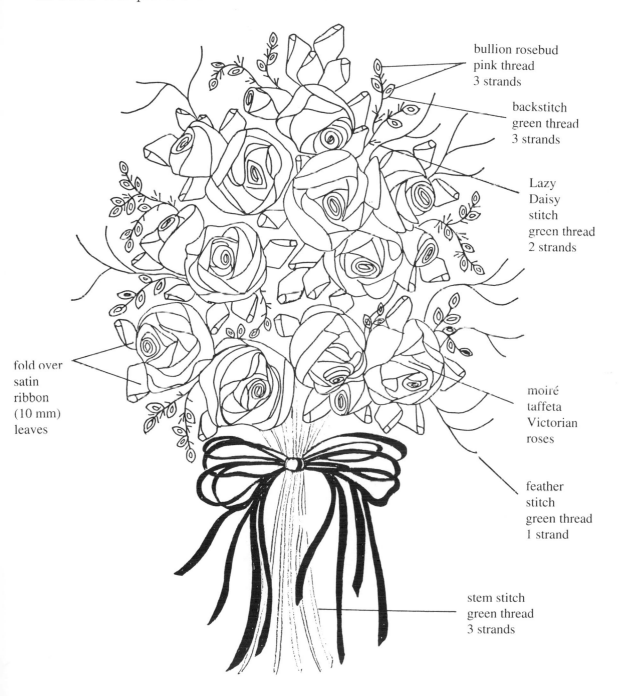

bullion rosebud
pink thread
3 strands

backstitch
green thread
3 strands

Lazy
Daisy
stitch
green thread
2 strands

fold over
satin
ribbon
(10 mm)
leaves

moiré
taffeta
Victorian
roses

feather
stitch
green thread
1 strand

stem stitch
green thread
3 strands

This stunning White wedding gown has been enhanced with clusters of satin ribbon roses, using the "two-tone" method in 25mm satin ribbon. The leaves have been made out of the dress fabric. The wedding gown belongs to Jodie Texeila and was made by Barbara & Zanne Koenig of the Bazatti Studio, Johannesburg.

This country-style wedding dress has been decorated with multi-coloured roses made from netting in the "two-tone" rose method. Clusters of pearls have been attached to the centre of the roses. The roses were made by Anne-Marie Shaw for her daughter's wedding.

This strapless wedding dress has been encrusted with satin ribbon roses using the "Victorian" rose technique in 14mm white satin ribbon. The wedding gown belongs to Carol-Ann Seara and was made by Barbara & Zanne Koenig of the Bazatti Studio, Johannesburg.